Sound Steps to Reading

Advanced Code

Diane McGuinness, Ph.D.

www.trafford.com

North America & international
toll-free: 1 888 232 4444 (USA & Canada)
fax: 812 355 4082

Workbook: Table of Contents

Table of Contents, page 2

Compound Words. Worksheet 1

Use the word '**sun**' or the word '**fire**' to make a new word.

_____fly   _____day

_____shine   _____wood

_____side   _____set

_____wood   _____drill

_____dress   _____dial

_____man   _____rise

_____flower   _____works

_____place   _____light

Compound Words. Worksheet 2

Use the word **'land'** or **'house'** to make a new word.

up_____   _____hold

farm_____   _____mine

dog_____   _____work

marsh_____   _____fill

low_____   _____wife

play_____

school_____

high_____

tree_____

wet_____

steak_____

Compound Words. Worksheet 3

Use the word 'light' or 'line' to make a new word.

air_____

head_____

day_____

dead_____

fire_____

sun_____

base_____

spot_____

flash_____

coast_____

clothes_____

moon_____

Compound Words. Worksheet 4

Mix and Match: Choose a word from the list on the right to make a new word with the words on the left.

after_____   **cake**

bus_____   **road**

cup_____   **stack**

cow_____   **noon**

fish_____   **car**

hay_____   **fly**

hair_____   **fold**

street_____   **dog**

witch_____   **hook**

rail_____   **bridge**

toe_____   **stop**

earth_____   **craft**

blind_____   **boy**

draw_____   **brush**

butter_____   **quake**

hot_____   **nail**

Homophones. Worksheet 5.

Some words sound the same but have different meanings. These words usually have different spellings. Circle the letters that stand for the **vowels** in each pair of words.

lead	led	beech	beach
vale	veil	meet	meat
herd	heard	threw	through
boar	bore	teem	team
wear	where	doe	dough
whir	were	seam	seem
war	wore	loan	lone
fare	fair	know	no
gait	gate	bough	bow
grate	great	piece	peace
one	won	buy	by
earn	urn	strait	straight
fur	fir	weather	whether

Homophones. Worksheet 6

Each sentence contains a pair of homophones from Worksheet 5.   Write the words in the right place so the sentence makes sense.

heard   herd

John _____ a _____ of goats in the grove.

boar   bore

Chasing wild _____ is never a _____.

wear   where

_____ shall I _____ my new suit?

war   wore

The nurses _____ white uniforms in the _____.

bear   bare

The grizzly _____ stood up on a _____ rock.

gate   gait

The horse quickened his _____ as he reached the _____.

straight   strait

The ship steered _____ as it sailed through the_____.

great   grate

The fire in the _____ looked _____.

won   one

There was only _____ who _____ the race.

urn earn

I don't _____ enough money to buy that pretty _____.

fur fir

The hunters saw some _____ on the bark of a _____.

weather whether

We don't know _____ the _____ will be fine.

meat meet

The butcher went to _____ the man who sells _____.

seem seam

The tailor sewed each _____ so it would _____ perfect.

through threw

Jim _____ the rock _____ the air.

doe dough

A pie crust is made of _____, but a lady deer is a _____.

no know

There is _____ one I _____ who goes to this school.

peace piece

Each child got a _____, so now there was _____.

Special Plurals. Worksheet 7

Adding plurals to nouns ending in the sound /f/

All these words end in the sound /f/ (spelled **f** or **ff** or **ph** or **gh**). Make each word plural.   Sometimes you add **s.** Sometimes you drop **f** and add **ves.** Decide which is right by **listening** as you say each word out loud. Write the correct answer next to the word.

elf _____ elves ____

calf _____

dwarf _____

cliff _____

shelf _____

chief _____

hoof _____

knife _____

laugh _____

leaf _____

wolf _____

life _____

loaf _____

shelf _____

graph _____

Adding Suffixes. Worksheet 8

Verbs with the sound /ae/ spelled <u>a-e</u>

Change each word by adding **ing** then **ed.** Drop the letter **e** at the end of each word. The suffix **ing** stands for ongoing action. The suffix **ed** stands for doing something in the past.

	ing	ed
bake	baking	baked
blaze		
brake		
care		
chase		
date		
engage		
escape		
fade		
frame		
graze		
hate		
pace		
paste		
race		
skate		
wave		

Adding Suffixes. Worksheet 9

Verbs with the sound /ie/ spelled <u>i-e</u>

Change each word by adding **ing** then **ed**. Drop the letter **e** at the end of each word. The suffix **ing** stands for ongoing action. The suffix **ed** stands for doing something in the past.

	ing	ed
arrive		
aspire		
chime		
dine		
file		
glide		
guide		
hike		
inspire		
like		
shine		
slice		
smile		
thrive		
whine		
wipe		

Adding Suffixes. Worksheet 10

Verbs with the sound /oe/ spelled o-e

Change each word by adding **ing** then **ed**. Drop the letter **e** at the end of each word. The suffix **ing** stands for ongoing action. The suffix **ed** stands for doing something in the past.

	ing	ed
adore		
choke		
close		
cope		
doze		
evoke		
hope		
ignore		
joke		
mope		
phone		
poke		
quote		
rave		
snore		
stroke		
vote		

Adding Suffixes. Worksheet 11.

Verbs with the sound /ue/ spelled <u>u-e</u>

Change each word by adding **ing** then **ed**. Drop the letter **e** at the end of each word. The suffix **ing** stands for ongoing action. The suffix **ed** stands for doing something in the past.

	ing	ed
abuse		
accuse		
amuse		
argue		
compute		
cure		
dispute		
endure		
fuse		
insure		
muse		
refuse		
refute		
use		

Adding Suffixes. Worksheet 12
Verbs with the vowel sound /a/

Change each word by adding **ing** then **ed**. Keep the vowel sound the same by doubling the last consonant. Then add the suffix.

	ing	**ed**
bat	batting	batted
brag		
chat		
clap		
cram		
flap		
grab		
jab		
lag		
lap		
pat		
plan		
slam		
slap		
snap		
stab		
trap		
wrap		

Adding Suffixes. Worksheet 13

Verbs with the vowel sound /e/

Change each word by adding **ing** then **ed**. Keep the vowel sound the same by doubling the last consonant. Then add the suffix.

	ing	**ed**

beg _____

excel _____

fret _____

hem _____

net _____

pen _____

pet _____

shed _____

shred _____

sled _____

spell _____

stem _____

step _____

web _____

wed _____

Adding Suffixes. Worksheet 14

Verbs with the vowel sound /i/

Change each word by adding **ing** or **ed**. Keep the vowel sound the same by doubling the last consonant. Then add the suffix.

	ing	ed
brim		
clip		
dip		
drip		
flit		
grin		
grip		
pin		
pit		
quip		
rip		
sin		
skid		
skim		
spin		
swim		
trim		
whip		

Adding Suffixes. Worksheet 15

Verbs with the vowel sound /o/

Change each word by adding **ing** then **ed**. Keep the vowel sound the same by doubling the last consonant. Then add the suffix.

	ing	ed
bob		
blot		
chop		
clog		
clot		
dot		
drop		
hop		
jog		
mop		
plot		
rot		
rob		
sob		
shop		
stop		
trot		

Adding Suffixes. Worksheet 16
Verbs with the vowel sound /u/

Change each word by adding **ing** then **ed**. Keep the vowel sound the same by doubling the last consonant. Then add the suffix.

	ing	ed
club		
cup		
drum		
gun		
hum		
hug		
plug		
rub		
shrug		
shut		
slug		
stun		
tug		
thud		

Adding Suffixes. Worksheet 17

Verbs ending in the sounds /th/ and /v/

Words that end in the sounds /th/ and /v/ are spelled **the** and **ve.** Drop the final **e** before adding the suffixes **ing** and **ed**.

	ing	ed
arrive		
bathe		
breathe		
carve		
clothe		
curve		
live		
love		
move		
pave		
prove		
save		
solve		
soothe		
strive		
writhe		

Adding Suffixes. Worksheet 18

Verbs ending in the sound /j/

The sound /j/ is always spelled **ge** or **dge** at the ends of words. Drop the final **e** before you add the suffixes **ing** and **ed**.

	ing	**ed**
bulge		
change		
charge		
cringe		
damage		
dodge		
edge		
forage		
hedge		
judge		
lunge		
pledge		
plunge		
rage		
stage		
surge		
urge		

Adding Suffixes. Worksheet 19

Multi-syllable verbs ending in the sounds /ul/

In these words the sounds /ul/ are spelled more than one way. Keep the same vowel sound when adding a suffix by dropping the final **e**. Final consonants do not have to be doubled in these words.

	ing	ed
amble		
cancel		
cuddle		
dazzle		
dribble		
fumble		
huddle		
hustle		
label		
marvel		
mumble		
pedal		
scramble		
signal		
struggle		
tangle		
travel		

Adding Suffixes. Worksheet 20

Verbs ending in the sound /ee/

In multi-syllable words, the final sound /ee/ is usually spelled **y**. Here are some two-syllable verbs ending in the sound /ee/. Nothing changes when you add the suffix **ing.** Change **y** to **i** when you add the suffix **ed**.

	ing	**ed**
bully	bullying	bullied
bury		
carry		
dally		
ferry		
hurry		
marry		
pity		
scurry		
tally		
worry		

Adding Suffixes. Worksheet 21

Verbs ending in the sound /ie/

To add suffixes to these verbs, notice whether the /ie/ sound is spelled **y** or **ie**.

	ing	ed
cry	crying	cried
defy		
dry		
fly		
fry		
pry		
spy		
try		
supply		
terrify		
die	dying	died
lie		
tie		
vie		
untie		

Adding Suffixes. Worksheet 22

Add the sound /ee/ to make an adjective

You can change words into adjectives by adding the sound /ee/ - spelled **y**. 1) Drop the final **e** before you add **y**. 2) Double the final consonant **if** the letter **y** changes the vowel sound.

babe sun breeze brine cloud cat blur craze curl ease

edge foam fun fur gloom hair health ice luck mist mud

run rust salt scare shade slime smell soap spot squeak

star oil steam thorn touch trust wave wind wit wool

baby_____   _____   _____

sunny_____   _____   _____

_____   _____   _____

_____   _____   _____

_____   _____   _____

_____   _____   _____

_____   _____   _____

_____   _____   _____

_____   _____   _____

_____   _____   _____

_____   _____   _____

_____   _____   _____

Adding Suffixes. Worksheet 23

Turning verbs into 'persons'

Change these verbs into 'persons' by adding the suffix <u>er</u>. Drop final <u>e</u>. Double the last consonant **IF** the suffix changes the vowel sound.

er

bake <u>   baker   </u>

call _____

drum _____

dive _____

farm _____

fiddle _____

follow _____

hack _____

jog _____

kill _____

pot _____

rob _____

run _____

ride _____

sell _____

shop _____

win _____

Adding Suffixes. Worksheet 24

Suffix potluck

Here is a list of suffixes. See how many of them you can add to each word to make new words.

able   ance   ed   en   er   est   ful   ing   ish   less   ly   ment   ness

bright _____

pity _____

fresh _____

care _____

turn _____

fine _____

face _____

pose _____

enjoy _____

excite _____

hope _____

happy _____

able ance ed en er est ful ing ish less ly ment ness

fool _____

sad _____

dirty _____

move _____

form _____

like _____

state _____

cheer _____

wonder _____

base _____

kind _____

firm _____

place _____

clean _____

Adjacent Vowel Sounds. Worksheet 25

Two-syllable words

These words have two vowel sounds side-by-side. Each vowel counts as one syllable. Read the word out loud and draw a slash between each syllable. Copy each word with a line between each syllable.   The letter **i** stands for **/ie/** (tie) in the first syllable in these words.

po/et   client   fuel   briar   ruin   dial   trial   giant   diet

vial   cruel   friar   pliant   riot   quiet   triumph   create

truant   chaos   poem   loyal   lion   fluid   duel   fluent

_____po--et_____

_____   _____

_____   _____

_____   _____

_____   _____

_____   _____

_____   _____

_____   _____

_____   _____

_____   _____

_____   _____

Adding Prefixes. Worksheet 26

de against, undo, entirely   **re** do again

Add one of these prefixes to these words or 'roots' to make new words.
Sometimes both prefixes are correct.

_____bate   _____deem

_____claim   _____cover

_____mand   _____tain

_____late   _____lay

_____feat   _____store

_____cite   _____fend

_____vour   _____main

_____peat   _____trieve

_____store   _____coy

_____move   _____mind

_____velop   _____cember

_____pose   _____pair

_____cay   _____clare

_____press   _____cent

Adding Prefixes. Worksheet 27

pre before, ahead of time   **pro** for, in favor of

Add one of these prefixes to these words or 'roots' to make new words.
Sometimes both prefixes are correct.

_____tend	_____file
_____pose	_____gram
_____long	_____cise
_____vent	_____mote
_____claim	_____nounce
_____ceed	_____fer
_____duce	_____pare
_____view	_____found
_____fess	_____tect
_____dict	_____cook
_____sent	_____test
_____vide	_____heat
_____voke	_____tect

Adding Prefixes. Worksheet 28

be at, near, around   **e** out, out of, from

Add one of these prefixes to these words or 'roots' to make new words.

_____ware   _____low

_____namel   _____come

_____side   _____voke

_____ven   _____hind

_____long   _____quip

_____ternal   _____neath

_____fore   _____hold

_____tween   _____vict

_____ject   _____sides

_____mit   _____tray

_____vent   _____lect

Adding Prefixes. Worksheet 29

im   **in**   not, in, into

Add one of these prefixes to these words or 'roots' to make new words.
'im' usually comes before **m** and **p**.

_____perfect   _____polite

_____struct   _____pure

_____pair   _____fer

_____side   _____sure

_____doors   _____pale

_____form   _____ward

_____ply   _____mune

_____trude   _____vite

_____pact   _____press

_____portant   _____vent

_____vest   _____prove

_____mense   _____sight

_____stinct   _____possible

Adding Prefixes. Worksheet 30

em   **en**   in, into, upon, cause to be

Add one of these prefixes to these words or 'roots' to make new words.
'em' usually comes before **b** and **p**.

_____**bark**   _____**act**

_____**noble**   _____**rage**

_____**barrass**   _____**ber**

_____**force**   _____**ploy**

_____**brace**   _____**joy**

_____**large**   _____**broider**

_____**peror**   _____**gage**

_____**ploy**   _____**pire**

_____**trust**   _____**blem**

_____**phasize**   _____**list**

Adjacent Vowel Sounds. Worksheet 31

Three syllable words

These words have two vowel sounds side-by-side. Read the word out loud.
Mark syllable boundaries as shown. Underline the strong syllable. Copy each
word as shown. The letter **i** can stand for the sounds /ee/ /ie/ or /i/.

<u>de</u>/i/ty violin denial chariot radio stadium idea

piety violent defiant oasis annual dialect peony

orient reliant trivial medium diary studio museum

pioneer usual zodiac alien idiot cereal diagram

_____ de--i--ty ____ _____ _____

_____ _____ _____

_____ _____ _____

_____ _____ _____

_____ _____ _____

_____ _____ _____

_____ _____ _____

_____ _____ _____

_____ _____ _____

_____ _____ _____

Multi-syllable Words Ending <u>ine</u>. Worksheet 32

Vowel controlled sort.

The letters <u>i-e</u> in <u>ine</u> stands for either /**ee**/ in 'seen,' /**ie**/ in 'tie' and /**i**/ in 'pin' in these words. Mark syllable boundaries. Underline the strong syllable. Copy each word under the vowel sound for how '**ine**' sounds in the word. Clue: The position of the strong syllable affects the vowel sound in <u>ine</u>.

ma/<u>chine</u> routine famine gasoline medicine genuine refine

magazine doctrine porcupine routine tangerine margarine

masculine turpentine marine sardine define discipline ravine

routine nectarine feminine undermine determine submarine

/ee/	/ie/	/i/
machine	refine	famine

Multi-syllable Words Ending <u>ite</u> or <u>ice</u>. Worksheet 33

Vowel controlled sort.

Mark syllable boundaries. Underline the strong syllable. Copy each word under the correct heading for the vowel sound in the final syllable. Clue: The position of the strong syllable affects the vowel sound in these endings.

<u>de</u>/fin/ite appetite favorite elite infinite recite satellite

opposite parasite excite petite polite expedite

malice police justice practice office

caprice notice service crevice novice

/ee/	/ie/	/i/
_____	_____	_____
_____	_____	_____
_____	_____	_____
_____	_____	_____
_____	_____	_____
_____	_____	_____
_____	_____	_____
_____	_____	_____
_____	_____	_____
_____	_____	_____

Multi-syllable Words Ending in a Schwa. Worksheet 34

When a word ends in a 'schwa,' it is spelled with the letter **a**. Mark syllable boundaries. Underline the strong syllable in the word.

<u>tu</u>/ba cinema soda diploma sofa aroma gala hyena

antenna polka villa camera drama opera comma

tuna orchestra umbrella zebra cobra quota magenta

veranda vanilla banana lava siesta extra lava aroma

formula azalea saliva data plaza gorilla pajama era

camera aroma veranda hula llama idea puma

Here is a start on a list of names of states that end a schwa. See if you can finish the list.

Alabama Alaska _____

_____

_____

Unscrambling Schwas and Prefixes. Worksheet 35

Many words start with the letter **a**. Sometimes it stands for a schwa. Sometimes it forms a prefix with the next letter (**ab**). Say each word out loud and **listen**. Mark the syllable boundaries **the way you hear them**. (Double consonants are usually one sound). Underline the main syllable. Circle the letter **a** if it's a schwa, but not if it isn't.

a/<u>bate</u>   <u>ab</u>/sent   abolish   abnormal   absolute   aboard

ability   absorb   about   abduct   abstract   abuse   ablaze

absurd   abroad   abstain   abrupt   abominable   above

a/<u>cad</u>/e/my   a/<u>ccount</u>   across   accuse   actual   acclaim

acoustic   acrobat   actor   accompany   access   acquire

accept   accost   accomplice   acute   accident   active

Unscrambling Schwas and Prefixes. Worksheet 36

Follow the directions for Worksheet 35.

a/<u>dore</u> <u>ad</u>/mi/ral adjective adult advantage adopt

adrift admire advertise adept address advance

admit adjourn adorn administer adverb advise

aflame affect affair afford afoot after

affix affront afraid affirm affable afflict

alarm alight allow almond along aloud

also alike album alley alert almost altar

although alas allege almond alive alibi

alphabet alone always alligator alternate

Unscrambling Schwas and Prefixes. Worksheet 37

Follow the directions for Worksheet 35.

amount   amber   ambulance   amuse   amok

America   amateur   ambush   amaze   ample

amble   among   amend   ample   amiss   amethyst

announce   anchovy   answer   antelope   annoy

another   animal   annual   anthem   antique   anew

annex   antler   antic   anniversary   anatomy

apart   apparent   apathy   apple   apology

appetite   appear   apply   apostle   approve

appoint   approach   apartment   applaud   appeal

Unscrambling Schwas and Prefixes. Worksheet 38

Follow the directions for Worksheet 35

arena   around   arcade   arrange   artist   arise

arrest   argue   aroma   army   armor   arithmetic

arrive   arsenic   article   array   arouse   artichoke

assault   assert   aspirin   assist   astonish

assume   ascend   assess   aspire   asleep

assassin   asphalt   aside   aspect   astute   assembly

attach   attack   atlas   atom   attempt   attic   attend

attain   attract   attitude   attorney   atmosphere

avail   avalanche   avoid   average   avenue   avenge

await   award   awake   away

Multi-syllable Words Ending ate. Worksheet 39

The ending 'ate' can stand for 'ut' (a schwa) **or** 'ate' (as in 'date'.). Copy the words in the correct column. Then mark syllable boundaries and underline the strong syllable.

senate   private   vibrate   educate   delicate   accurate   hesitate

pirate   immediate   liberate   frustrate   desolate   demonstrate

fortunate   corporate   dictate   evaporate   adequate   concentrate

/ut/	/ate/
se/nate	vi/brate

Adding Suffixes. Worksheet 40

Change verbs into nouns with merri-'ment'

The suffix 'ment' is always on a weak syllable and sounds 'munt' (a schwa).
Turn these verbs into nouns by adding **ment**. Root word stays the same, except
drop <u>e</u> in 'argue.' Mark syllable boundaries. Underline the strong syllable.

achieve _____	accomplish _____	adjust _____
advance _____	agree _____	announce _____
argue _____	assign _____	astonish _____
attach _____	attain _____	command _____
commence _____	detach _____	develop _____
employ _____	enjoy _____	equip _____
excite _____	improve _____	invest _____
manage _____	measure _____	move _____
pave _____	place _____	refresh _____
punish _____	require _____	state _____

Adding Suffixes. Worksheet 41

Create adjectives and nouns by adding <u>ive</u>

The suffix <u>ive</u> is always a weak syllable and sounds 'uv' (a schwa). Turn these words into adjectives or nouns by adding <u>ive</u>. Root word stays the same, except drop final **e** from words. Mark syllable boundaries and underline the strong syllable.

act _____   assert _____   attract _____

collect _____   construct _____   cooperate _____

correct _____   create _____   defect _____

detect _____   digest _____   distinct _____

effect _____   execute _____   invent _____

narrate _____   object _____   operate _____

percept _____   prevent _____   protect _____

reflect _____   restrict _____   secret _____

select _____   subject _____   suggest _____

aggress _____   abuse _____   excess _____

expanse _____   expense _____   express _____

impress _____   impulse _____   offense _____

oppress _____   progress _____   repulse _____

response _____   success _____

Adding Suffixes. Worksheet 42

Adding <u>ive</u> when root word has to change

Changing these words isn't so easy. For the words on the left, drop **de** and add **sive**. For the "bonus" words, there is no simple answer. Say the words out loud as you work. Mark syllable boundaries and underline the strong syllable.

Adding 'sive'	**Bonus Words**
conclude _con/clu/sive_	add _add/i/tive_
corrode _____	adhere _____
decide _____	attend _____
delude _____	cohere _____
elude _____	compete _____
evade _____	conserve _____
exclude _____	deceive _____
explode _____	destroy _____
include _____	permit _____
intrude _____	retain _____
persuade _____	sense _____
protrude _____	submit _____

The Latin Suffix 'us'. Worksheet 43

The suffix **ous** makes an adjective meaning 'full of." It is always a weak syllable and **ou** is a schwa.   Mark syllable boundaries. Underline the strong syllable.

Two/three syllable words

marvelous frivolous fabulous pendulous obvious envious

perilous populous famous blasphemous stupendous serious

porous grievous numerous humorous riotous hazardous

hideous piteous ravenous ominous gluttonous slanderous

ponderous murderous generous prosperous dubious tedious

odious studious glorious furious curious ruinous dangerous

vigorous glamorous rapturous arduous strenuous jealous

pompous wondrous monstrous nervous enormous disastrous

Four/five syllable words

impervious mischievous superfluous magnanimous oblivious

conspicuous ambiguous continuous impetuous simultaneous

amphibious fastidious miscellaneous instantaneous miraculous

Spell Sort. Find the vowel letter that stands for a schwa.

There is one schwa in each word. Mark syllable boundaries. Underline the strong syllable. Circle the schwa. Write each word under the correct vowel letter for the <u>spelling of the schwa</u>.

hesitate benefit reliant gratify impolite satellite cultivate

dominate economy piracy dialect possible aspirin antelope

animate custody appetite paragraph arithmetic paradise

melody privacy artichoke parasite terrible pacify congregate

a	e	i	o
		hesitate	

The Latin suffix 'shun' spelled <u>tion</u>. Worksheet 45

Write the whole word. Make nouns by adding <u>tion</u> to these words. Drop the final
<u>t</u> in the root word.

adopt	adoption	**assert**
attract		**collect**
corrupt		**deduct**
distinct		**edit**
elect		**except**
exhibit		**extinct**
inhibit		**insert**
instruct		**invent**
object		**obstruct**
perfect		**predict**
prevent		**reject**
select		**suggest**

The Latin Suffix 'shun' spelled <u>tion</u>. Worksheet 46

Write the whole word. Make nouns by adding <u>tion</u>. Drop the letters <u>te</u> from the root word first.

abbreviate abbreviation	**abdicate**
accelerate	**accumulate**
agitate	**alternate**
animate	**anticipate**
appreciate	**approximate**
automate	**calculate**
celebrate	**circulate**
collaborate	**communicate**
compensate	**complicate**
concentrate	**confiscate**
congratulate	**congregate**
contemplate	**cooperate**
corporate	**create**

cultivate   decorate

dedicate   deflate

delegate   demonstrate

desolate   devastate

dictate   discriminate

dominate   donate

educate   elevate

emancipate   emigrate

estimate   evacuate

fascinate   fixate

frustrate   graduate

hesitate   humiliate

illustrate   imitate

immigrate   implicate

indicate   inflate

integrate	insulate
investigate	irrigate
irritate	isolate
legislate	liberate
locate	manipulate
migrate	narrate
negate	nominate
operate	participate
populate	radiate
recreate	relate
rotate	segregate
separate	speculate
stimulate	suffocate
tabulate	tolerate
translate	vacate

The Latin suffix 'shun' spelled <u>tion</u>. Worksheet 47.

Write the whole word. Make nouns by adding <u>tion</u>. Change final <u>e</u> to <u>a</u> first.

accuse   accusation   admire

adore   centralize

characterize   civilize

colonize   combine

condense   conserve

converse   declare

derive   determine

examine   explore

fertilize   generalize

illumine   imagine

improvise   incline

inflame   invite

inspire   mature

oblige

observe

organize

prepare

preserve

quote

realize

recite

reserve

restore

sense

starve

The Latin Suffix 'shun' spelled <u>tion</u>. Worksheet 48.

Write the whole word. Make nouns by adding <u>tion</u>. **Add the letter <u>a</u> before <u>tion</u>.**

adapt	adaptation	**affect**	
affirm		**alien**	
assassin		**cancel**	
condemn		**confirm**	
consider		**consult**	
expect		**experiment**	
export		**flirt**	
form		**habit**	
import		**inform**	
install		**interpret**	
limit		**liquid**	
plant		**pollen**	

present

recommend

resign

tempt

transport

protest

relax

tax

transform

The Latin Suffix 'shun' Spelled <u>tion</u>. Worksheet 49.

Write the whole word. These are uncommon forms. Follow the pattern set by the first example.

amplify   amplification   classify

fortify   gratify

identify   justify

modify   multiply

notify   purify

qualify

constitute constitution   contribute

distribute   electrocute

execute   institute

resolute   substitute

compose	composition	**depose**
dispose		**expose**
impose		**oppose**
propose		**transpose**

absorb	absorption	**assume**
conceive	conception	**deceive**
describe		**inscribe**
receive		**subscribe**
transcribe		

absolve	absolution	**convolve**
devolve		**dissolve**
evolve		**resolve**
revolve		**solve**

The Latin Suffix 'shun' Spelled t<u>ion</u>: Bonus Words

These have irregular spellings. Say the words before you write them.

abstain	abstention	**attend**
contain		**contend**
declaim		**despair**
detain		**exclaim**
explain		**extend**
intend		**pretend**
proclaim		**pronounce**
register		**repeat**
retain		

Word Lists

The Suffix 'er'

The suffix 'er' is common in many languages. It is spelled <u>er</u> most of the time, except in these Latin and Old French words.

ar   altar angular beggar burglar calendar caterpillar cedar cellar cellular circular collar cougar dollar familiar grammar granular hangar liar lunar molar mortar muscular nectar particular peculiar pillar polar poplar popular regular scholar similar solar sugar vinegar vulgar

'er' is spelled <u>ar</u> in these words too:

ard   awkward backward blizzard buzzard coward forward inward hazard leopard lizard mallard mustard orchard outward standard wizard

or   actor ambassador anchor armor author bachelor captor color condor conductor contractor debtor director doctor donor editor educator emperor endeavor error factor favor flavor harbor honor horror humor inspector instructor investor janitor juror labor manor major meteor minor mirror monitor motor neighbor odor operator pastor professor razor realtor rigor rumor sailor savor scissors sculptor senator senior spectator splendor sponsor squalor suitor superior supervisor tailor tenor terror tractor traitor tremor tutor valor vapor vendor victor vigor visitor visor warrior

Words ending in the sounds 'ater'

a-tor   accelerator administrator alligator aviator calculator collaborator commentator creator decorator dictator educator elevator generator illustrator imitator indicator legislator navigator operator radiator refrigerator speculator ventilator

The Suffix 'airy'

Spell this Latin suffix two ways.

ary   adversary arbitrary commentary contrary customary

culinary emissary honorary itinerary literary luminary

mercenary military missionary momentary monetary

necessary ordinary planetary sanctuary secondary

secretary sedentary seminary solitary tributary voluntary

unitary

ery   cemetery dysentery monastery presbytery

The Suffixes 'unt' and 'unce'

In these French suffixes, the schwa is spelled <u>a</u> or <u>e</u>. This spelling stays constant when adjectives (ant, ent) change to nouns (ance, ence).

ant   abundant adamant assistant blatant brilliant combatant constant defendant defiant distant elegant entrant expectant ignorant important informant instant irrelevant observant peasant pheasant pleasant recalcitrant redundant relevant reliant reluctant servant tenant valiant

ance   abundance allowance appearance assistance avoidance brilliance defiance distance elegance entrance expectance ignorance importance instance irrelevance observance parlance performance recalcitrance relevance reliance reluctance valiance

Words ending <u>ment</u> are not included.

ent   absent accident affluent apparent benevolent client competent consistent convenient convent crescent current deferent different deficient event evident expedient fervent indulgent ingredient innocent insistent intelligent intent invent lenient magnificent malevolent negligent obedient permanent persistent present president prevent prominent redolent referent resident reverent silent transparent turbulent violent

ence   absence accidence affluence audience benevolence competence conference consistence convenience deference difference essence evidence expedience experience indulgence influence innocence insistence intelligence interference lenience magnificence malevolence negligence obedience occurrence permanence persistence presence prominence redolence reference residence reverence science sentence silence transparence turbulence violence

The Latin Suffix 'shun'

This suffix is spelled <u>tion</u> most of the time. But there are the six other ways to spell it. <u>cian</u> is for an occupation or person. The last two words are Old French.

sion   accession admission aggression apprehension ascension commission compassion comprehension compression compulsion concession concussion condescension confession convulsion declension depression digression dimension discussion dissension emission emulsion expansion expression expulsion extension fission impression intermission mansion mission obsession omission oppression passion pension percussion permission possession pretension procession profession progression propulsion recession regression remission repulsion revulsion secession session submission succession suppression suspension tension transgression transmission

cian   academician beautician clinician electrician logician magician mathematician mortician musician obstetrician optician patrician pediatrician physician politician statistician technician

tian   dietitian gentian Martian titian

cion   coercion suspicion

cean   crustacean ocean

shion   cushion fashion

The Latin Suffixes 'shul' and 'shuh'

In these suffixes, /sh/ is spelled <u>ti</u> <u>ci</u> <u>si.</u>

tial   circumstantial confidential deferential differential essential experiential impartial influential initial martial palatial partial potential providential residential reverential sequential spatial substantial tangential

cial   artificial beneficial commercial crucial facial financial glacial judicial official prejudicial provincial racial sacrificial social special superficial

sial   controversial

The suffix /shu/ has only one spelling:

cia   acacia inertia militia minutia

This expands to /shee-ate/ in these words:

ciate   appreciate associate depreciate dissociate emaciate excruciating

The Latin Suffix 'shus'

In this suffix, the sound /sh/ is added to suffix <u>ous</u>. The sound /sh/ is spelled: <u>ci</u> <u>ti</u> <u>sci</u> <u>ce</u> <u>xi</u>.

cious   atrocious audacious auspicious avaricious capacious capricious delicious efficacious fallacious ferocious gracious judicious loquacious malicious mendacious meretricious officious pernicious perspicacious precious precocious pugnacious rapacious sagacious salacious spacious specious suspicious tenacious vicious vivacious voracious

tious   adventitious ambitious captious cautious conscientious contentious expeditious facetious factious fictitious fractious licentious nutritious ostentatious pretentious propitious repetitious seditious sententious superstitious surreptitious tendentious vexatious

scious   conscious luscious

ceous   curvaceous herbaceous

xious   anxious noxious obnoxious

The Latin Suffixes 'shunt' and 'shunce'

In these Latin Suffixes, the sound /sh/ is spelled <u>ci</u> <u>ti</u> <u>sci</u>.

cient   efficient deficient coefficient sufficient insufficient proficient

tient   impatient patient quotient sentient

scient   omniscient prescient

science   conscience prescience omniscience

tience   impatience patience

Suffixes and Other Words With the Sound /zh/

The Latin suffix /zhun/ has three spellings.

sion   abrasion adhesion aversion cohesion collision collusion conclusion confusion conversion decision delusion derision diffusion diversion division effusion erosion evasion exclusion excursion explosion fusion illusion immersion incision inclusion incursion infusion intrusion invasion lesion occasion persuasion perversion precision profusion provision revision seclusion subdivision submersion supervision transfusion version vision television

sian   artesian Asian Parisian Persian Malaysian

tion   equation

These Latin and Greek words end in /zhuh/

sia   ambrosia amnesia anesthesia aphasia euthanasia fantasia Asia Persia Malaysia

French words with the sound /zh/

ge   barrage beige garage massage montage negligee prestige rouge sabotage camouflage

s(ure)   leisure measure pleasure treasure

s(u)   casual visual

Spelling the Sound /ch/ in Latin Words and Suffixes

/ch/ is spelled <u>ti</u>, <u>ci</u>, and <u>t</u>

'chun'/ 'chunt'

tion   bastion combustion congestion digestion exhaustion
question suggestion indigestion

tian   Christian

cient   ancient

'chul'

tial   credential presidential essential potential confidential providential

'chur'

ture   adventure agriculture aperture architecture capture caricature
conjecture creature culture curvature denture departure
expenditure feature fixture forfeiture fracture furniture future
gesture horticulture juncture lecture legislature literature
manufacture mature miniature mixture moisture nature nurture
overture pasture picture posture puncture rapture rupture
scripture sculpture signature structure temperature texture
torture venture vulture

'choo' The sounds /choo/ come in the middle of these words.

tu   accentuate actual actually century conceptual congratulate
constituent effectual estuary eventual factual fatuous flatulent
fluctuate fortune fortunate habitual habituate impetuous
infatuate intellectual mutual obituary perpetual perpetuate
petulant postulate presumptuous ritual sanctuary saturate
situate spatula statue stature statute sumptuous tarantula
tempestuous tortuous tumultuous virtual virtue virtuoso virtuous

Spelling the Sound /j/ in Latin/French Words

The sound /j/ is spelled <u>ge</u> or <u>gi.</u>

gious   contagious religious prodigious egregious sacrilegious

geous   advantageous courageous gorgeous outrageous

gion   contagion legion region religion

geon   surgeon pigeon dungeon bludgeon

Some Important Latin Roots

aud/audio	to hear, listen
cad/cas	to fall
cap/cep	to take, receive
capit/capt	head, chief
cede/ceed/cess	to go, yield, surrender
cern/cert	to decide, fix
cise/cide	to cut, kill
cred/credo	believe, belief
cur/curs	to run, to go, flow
dic/dict	to say, tell
duc/duce/duct	to lead, guide
fac/fact/fect	to make, to do
feder, fide, fid	trust, faith, faithful
fer	to bear, to carry
flect/flex	to bend
form/forma	to shape
gen/genus	race, species, kind, birth
grad/gress	to go, to walk
greg	group, crowd, herd
leg/legis	the law
leg/lect	to choose, pick, read
lit/littera	letters, written down
jac/jec/ject	to throw, to lie

mit/miss	to send
mob/mot/movere	to move
ped/pod	foot
pel/puls	to drive, push
pend/pens	to hang, weigh
pon/pose	to put, place, set
port	to carry
rupt	to break, burst
scrib/script	to write
spec/spect	to see, watch
spire/spire	to breathe
sta/stit/stet	to stand
stru/struct	to build
ten/tain	to hold
tend/tens/tent	to stretch, strain
tract	to pull
vert/vers	to turn
vis/vid	to see
viv/vit/vita	to live
voc/voca	voice, to speak

Some Important Latin and Greek Prefixes

ab	away from
ac, ad, af, ag **al, an, ap, ar,** **as, at,**	at, to, towards
ante	in front of
bene	well, good
bi, by	two
circum	around, circle
co, com, **con, cor**	with, together
de, di	undo, opposite to
dis	apart, reverse, remove
dys	sick, bad
e, en	in, into
ex	out, formerly
for	in front of
im, in	into in,
inter	between
intra	within
intro	into, inward
mal	bad
non	not
ob	in the way of, against, down
per	through
post	after
pre	before
pro	for, in favor of
re	do again
retro	go back, at the rear
sub	under, below
super	large
sur	above, on, go beyond
trans	across
tri	three
un	not, undo
uni	one

Common Greek Words and Spelling Patterns

The sound /k/

ch   ache anachronism anarchy anchor archeology architect archives chaos character chasm chemist chlorine choir chord choreography chorus Christ Christian Christmas chronic chronicle chronology echo epoch hierarchy mechanic melancholy monarch ocher orchestra parochial scheme scholar scholastic school stomach synchronize technical

The sound /i/ in the middle of words

y   abyss amethyst anonymous crypt crystal cylinder gymnasium hymn hypocrite hysteria idyll lynx martyr mystery mystify myth physics pygmy rhythm sycamore syllable syllabus sylvan symbol symmetry sympathy symphony symptom synchronize synopsis system typical

The sound /ie/ in the middle of words

y   cycle cyclone cypress dynamic dynamo gyrate gyroscope hydrant hydraulic hyphen typhoid typhoon tyrant xylophone

The sound /f/

ph   alphabet aphid asphalt atmosphere cipher elephant decipher dolphin emphasis geography graph hyphen metaphor morpheme orphan phantom pharmacy phase pheasant philosophy phobia phone phoneme photo phrase physical physician physics prophet saxophone symphony telephone topography typhoon trophy

The sound /n/
pn   pneumatic pneumonia

The sound /r/
rh   rhapsody rhetoric rheumatism rhinoceros rhomboid rhubarb rhyme rhythm

The sound /s/
ps   psalm pseudonym psyche psychology psychiatry

The sound /z/
x   xenon xerography xylophone

Greek Words for the Study of Knowledge

These words end in a form of the word 'logos' meaning knowledge of, or study of.

analogy anthology anthropology apology astrology biology

cardiology chronology cosmology criminology dermatology

epistemology ethnology etymology genealogy geology

gynecology ichthyology ideology meteorology methodology

mythology ontology ornithology paleontology pathology

psychology pharmacology physiology sociology technology

terminology theology typology zoology